Character Values

I Am
Polite

by Sarah L. Schuette

Consulting Editor: Gail Saunders-Smith, PhD
Consultant: Madonna Murphy, PhD
Professor of Education, University of St. Francis, Joliet, Illinois
Author, *Character Education in America's Blue Ribbon Schools*

Capstone
press

Mankato, Minnesota

Pebble Books are published by Capstone Press
151 Good Counsel Drive, P.O. Box 669, Mankato, Minnesota 56002
www.capstonepress.com

1 2 3 4 5 6 09 08 07 06 05 04

Library of Congress Cataloging-in-Publication Data
Schuette, Sarah L., 1976–
    I am polite / by Sarah L. Schuette.
    p. cm.—(Character values)
    Includes bibliographical references and index.
    ISBN 0-7368-2572-X (hardcover)
    1. Courtesy—Juvenile literature. [1. Etiquette.] I. Title. II. Series.
BJ1533.C9S38 2005
177′.1—dc22   2003024170

Summary: Simple text and photographs illustrate how children can be polite.

Note to Parents and Teachers

The Character Values series supports national social studies
standards for units on individual development and identity. This
book describes politeness and illustrates ways students can be
polite. The photographs support early readers in understanding
the text. The repetition of words and phrases helps early readers
learn new words. This book also introduces early readers to
subject-specific vocabulary words, which are defined in the
Glossary. Early readers may need assistance to read some words
and to use the Table of Contents, Glossary, Read More, Internet
Sites, and Index/Word List sections of the book.

Table of Contents

Being Polite

I am polite. I have good manners.

Polite Words

I say "thank you" to people who help me.

I say "hello" and shake hands with people I meet.

I say "excuse me"
after I sneeze.

12

I say "please"
when I ask for help.

Polite Actions

I pass food to other people first.

I answer the phone politely. I ask who is calling.

I write thank you notes for my gifts.

I am polite. I think
about the needs of others.

Glossary

gift—a present; people give each other gifts on special days like birthdays and holidays.

manners—the ways that people behave; people who think about the feelings of others have good manners.

note—a short letter or message

polite—well-behaved and courteous to others; another word for politeness is courtesy.

Read More

Amos, Janine. *After You.* Courteous Kids. Milwaukee: Gareth Stevens, 2001.

Doudna, Kelly. *Please.* Good Manners. Edina, Minn.: Abdo, 2001.

Leaney, Cindy. *It's Your Turn Now: A Story about Politeness.* Hero Club Character. Vero Beach, Fla.: Rourke Publishing, 2004.

Internet Sites

FactHound offers a safe, fun way to find Internet sites related to this book. All of the sites on FactHound have been researched by our staff.

Here's how:

1. Visit *www.facthound.com*
2. Type in this special code **073682572X** for age-appropriate sites. Or enter a search word related to this book for a more general search.
3. Click on the **Fetch It** button.

FactHound will fetch the best sites for you!

Index/Word List

Word Count: 76
Early-Intervention Level: 9

Editorial Credits

Mari C. Schuh, editor; Jennifer Bergstrom, series designer and illustrator; Enoch Peterson, book designer; Karen Hieb, product planning editor

Photo Credits

Capstone Press/Gem Photo Studio/Dan Delaney, all

The author dedicates this book to her friends at the Henderson Public Library in Henderson, Minnesota.